Holiday Crafts

Holiday
Crafts

35 projects for the
home and for giving

Catherine Woram

CICO BOOKS
LONDON NEW YORK

Published in 2013 by CICO Books
an imprint of Ryland Peters & Small
519 Broadway, 5th floor, New York NY 10012

www.rylandpeters.com

10 9 8 7 6 5 4 3 2 1

Text, design, and photography copyright
© CICO Books 2013

A CIP catalog record for this book is
available from the Library of Congress.

ISBN: 978 1 78249 057 9

Printed in China

Copy editor: Caroline West
Design: Louise Leffler
Photography: Caroline Arber
Stylist: Catherine Woram
Illustrator: Louise Turpin

For digital editions, visit
www.cicobooks.com/apps.php

Contents

Introduction

Christmas is, without doubt, my very favorite time of year. I love the cold weather—probably due to the fact that I am a winter baby! I adore decorating every nook and cranny of the house that I can. I've been creating decorations and beautiful objects for Christmas for as long as I can remember, and the chance to write a whole book on the subject was a major treat for me.

There is nothing more rewarding than making your very own Christmas decorations for the home, as well as crafting lovely gifts for your family and friends. From greetings cards and giftwrap ideas to suggestions for creating the most impressive table settings, this book is full of inspiration for the festive season. There are also simple makes for children who will, no doubt, enjoy every moment of creating gifts for friends and family, too.

Start by building up a craft box or cupboard at home and storing a variety of decorative items for creating your crafts. Keep a selection of glues, glitters, and decorative pens. Also try to save off-cuts of wrapping paper, ribbons, fabric, and Christmas cards to recycle into new decorations the following year, and forage for lovely buttons and braids in junk shops and sewing stores.

Whichever items you decide to make from the following pages for your Christmas, I do hope you have as much fun creating them as I did producing them for this book.

Wishing you a very merry Christmas!

Catherine Woram

Opposite: Felt tree decorations (see page 12)
Above: Miniature Christmas cakes (see page 94)

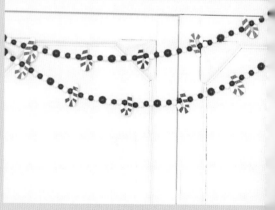

Chapter One
Decorations

Wooden bauble decorations

These simple little MDF decorations are painted in festive colors and decorated with rows of ric rac braid and miniature buttons, as well as tiny velvet bows, to create stylish decorations for your tree. You can opt for a traditional red and green color combination, which never fails to make an impact, or perhaps try using silver and gold instead.

Materials

MDF bauble shapes

Red and green acrylic paint

Paintbrush

Miniature velvet bow (or 4in/10cm of narrow velvet ribbon to make one)

Miniature buttons

Hot glue gun (or all-purpose glue)

Red, white, and green ric rac braid

Red cotton thread (to make the hanging loops)

Scissors

1 Paint the front and side edges of the MDF bauble and leave to dry completely. When the bauble is dry, turn it over and paint it on the other side. You may need to apply a second coat of paint if better coverage is required.

2 Glue the miniature velvet bow to the top of the decoration and add a row of tiny buttons along the central line of the painted decoration. You may find it easier to use a hot glue gun to do this if you have one.

3 Cut two lengths of ric rac braid to fit around both sides of the decoration. Glue the braid to the front and then fold the edges to the back. Glue in place and put an extra blob of glue on the ends of the braid to stop them fraying.

4 Cut a length of red cotton thread for the hanging loop, approximately 5in (13cm) long, and thread through the hole in the decoration. Tie the ends in a secure knot to finish.

Top tip

You can ring in the changes or make decorations to match your Christmas tree color scheme by using different paint colors and decorations. For instance, try adorning gold- and silver-painted baubles with gold and silver cup sequins and ric rac braid for a truly glamorous look.

Felt tree decorations

Dress a tree both effectively and inexpensively by making these decorative hearts, stars, and trees in plain felt with simple embroidered motifs finished with pearl buttons. Made in red, green, and white felt, these decorations feature a plain snowflake motif, worked in long and short running stitch, blanket-stitched edges, and a ribbon loop with which to hang them from the tree.

Materials

Tracing paper and pencil

Green, red, and white felt

Scissors

Pins, contrasting embroidery thread, and embroidery needle

Pearl buttons

6in (15cm) narrow ribbon (for the hanging loops)

Polyester batting (wadding) for the filling

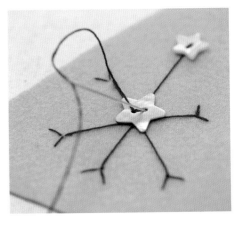

1 Using the templates on pages 122–23, trace the tree, star, and heart motifs onto the piece of paper with the pencil. Transfer your chosen motif to the green felt and cut out two shapes for each decoration. Draw the snowflake shape onto the front of one of the shapes with a soft pencil. Work the embroidery using long and short running stitch on the front of the decoration, following the design shown on the template.

2 Sew on one or two pearl buttons, depending on the design you've chosen. (In order to save time, you could stick the buttons on using a hot glue gun if you prefer.)

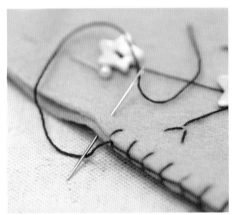

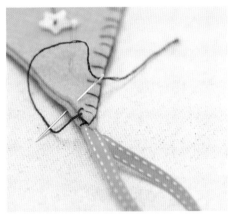

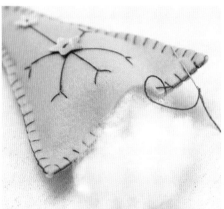

3 Pin the two shapes wrong sides together and begin to work blanket stitch around the edges using the embroidery thread. Start stitching along the bottom of the tree first so that the opening for the filling will be at the base of the decoration. Use small stitches, spaced approximately ¼in (5mm) apart.

4 Cut a length of narrow ribbon, approximately 4in (10cm) long, to make the hanging loop. Fold the ribbon in half and place the ends between the two layers of felt at the top of the tree. Continue blanket stitching around the tree, sandwiching the hanging loop between the felt as you stitch. In order to make the loop stronger, make a few extra stitches over the ribbon before continuing with the blanket stitch.

5 Continue to work the blanket stitch around the felt shape until you reach the bottom edge again and then leave an opening of around 2in (5cm) for the filling. Push the filling into the opening—you may find it easier to use the end of a pencil or knitting needle to do this. Fill the decoration well but do not overstuff. Sew up the opening at the bottom of the Christmas tree using blanket stitch to finish.

Gingham tree decorations

You can make these simple tree decorations in pretty red and green gingham fabric and then decorate them with lengths of ribbon to hang from your tree. You could also add some further embellishment in the form of tiny buttons and beads if you wish. If you have time, making enough of these decorations to cover your Christmas tree will create a really stylish look.

Materials

Tracing paper and pencil

Scissors

Pins

Red or green gingham fabric

12in (30cm) ribbon, approximately
½in (1cm) wide, for the decorative
trim and hanging loop

Needle and thread

Sewing machine

Polyester batting (wadding) for the
filling

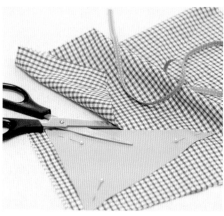

1 Using the template on page 122, trace the tree motif onto the piece of paper with the pencil. Cut out the tree template, pin it to the gingham fabric, and cut out the tree shape with the scissors. (Fold the fabric in half so that you can cut out two layers at a time.)

2 Lay the ribbon trim along the bottom straight edge of the tree on one layer of the fabric, about ¾in (2cm) from the edge, and stitch into position. You can either sew the ribbon to the fabric by hand or use the sewing machine.

3 With right sides facing stitch the tree shapes together using the sewing machine. Leave an opening of around 3in (8cm) on the bottom straight edge of the fabric to insert the filling. Trim and notch the corners of the fabric and turn to the right side. Cut a length of ribbon, measuring 4in (10cm), fold it in half, and stitch it to the top of the tree to form the hanging loop.

4 Insert the stuffing into the bottom of the tree shape. Use a pencil or knitting needle to push the stuffing inside the decoration. Stitch the opening closed by hand to finish.

Découpage letters

These plain papier mâché letters are découpaged with red-and-white gingham and polka-dot paper. The letters are then finished off with decorative bands of contrasting ric rac braid and tiny buttons to create these festive NOEL letters. They look striking lined up on a mantelpiece or table.

Materials

Old plate

Papier mâché letters (to spell Noel)

White or undercoat paint

Paintbrush

Scissors

Gingham and polka-dot design découpage paper

Découpage glue

Découpage varnish

White ric rac braid (enough to wrap around the sides of each letter)

Hot glue gun (or all-purpose glue)

Small red buttons (optional)

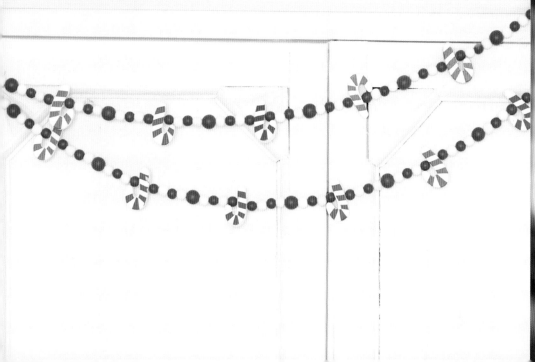

1 Working on an old plate, paint the letters with the white paint or undercoat, and leave to dry. This will prevent the brown papier mâché background from showing through. Paint all four of the letters and leave to dry thoroughly.

2 Use the scissors to cut the gingham and polka-dot paper into a collection of squares and rectangles, measuring between ¾–1¼in (2–3cm).

3 Stick a paper square or rectangle onto the letter by applying a thin layer of découpage glue to the letter and pressing the paper firmly into place. Continue to layer the paper around the letter, overlapping the pieces so that none of the background color shows through. Carefully fold the paper pieces over the curved edges of the letter shape. Leave to dry. Repeat for the rest of the letters.

4 Apply a thin coat of découpage varnish all over the letters, and leave them to dry thoroughly. If you wish, you can apply a further coat to make the letters more hard-wearing.

5 Cut a length of white ric rac braid to fit around the sides of each of the letters, and glue into position. You may find it easier to use a hot glue gun to do this. You can also decorate the sides of the letters with small red buttons.

Materials

Thin bendy twigs

Thin wire (preferably black)

White spray paint

Sharp scissors

Silver wire (to make the beaded hearts)

30 small red beads (for each of the beaded hearts)

Hot glue gun (or strong all-purpose glue)

5 wooden heart decorations

Artificial ivy leaves

Red ribbon bow

Fresh miniature ivy (to wind around the finished wreath)

Twiggy wreath with hearts and leaves

For a Christmas decoration that is really unusual, why not make your own door wreath out of some delicate garden twigs? The twigs are easily twisted into a circular shape, then spray them white to create a pretty wreath that will look just as good indoors as adorning your front door. The small beads that are used to make the red hearts look like tiny festive cranberries.

1 Bend the twigs round to form a circular shape and use short lengths of wire to keep them in place.

2 Spray the twigs with the white spray paint. You may need to do this in several stages to achieve full coverage. It's advisable to use the spray paint either outside or in a well-ventilated room.

3 Using scissors, cut a piece of silver wire approximately 6in (15cm) long and fold in half to form a V-shape. Thread 15 beads onto each end, then twist the ends several times to stop the beads falling off. Bend the ends of the wire down at the top to create the heart shape. Make four more beaded hearts for the wreath.

4 Use the thin wire to fix the beaded hearts around the wreath. Use the strong glue or a hot glue gun to stick the wooden heart decorations between each beaded heart. Tuck an artificial ivy leaf in the spaces between the hearts, using short pieces of wire to fix the leaves securely in place if you wish. Glue the red ribbon bow to the center of one of the wooden hearts.

5 Thread strands of fresh ivy around the wreath, tucking the ends into the twigs to keep them in position. Again, you may wish to use short pieces of wire to fix the ivy in place.

Dogwood wreath

With its gloriously deep shade of red, dogwood is the ideal choice for making a Christmas wreath and the twigs are fairly easy to bend into a circular shape. If you don't have any dogwood growing in your garden, then you should find that most florists' shops stock it. Decorated with pine cones and sprays of eucalyptus leaves, the wreath will look striking on any front door.

Materials

Garden cutters

Dogwood (*Cornus*) branches

Thin wire (for holding the branches in the wreath in place)

Scissors or small pair of pliers

Narrow green wire (for holding the pine cones in position)

Medium-sized pine cones

Branches of fresh eucalyptus

Sprigs of fresh rosemary

39in (1m) red gingham ribbon, 4in (10cm) wide, for hanging

1 Use the garden cutters to trim off the thicker ends of the dogwood branches, which are more difficult to twist than thinner ones. Tie a bunch of the branches together using a short length of wire and twist the ends of the wire together several times to hold the branches firmly in place.

2 Continue twisting the branches around to form the wreath shape and fix them into position with short lengths of wire.

Top tip

The winter garden contains many evergreen plants that can be used as indoor decorations. Here I used some sprigs of rosemary to add a finishing touch to my dogwood wreath. Yellow willow (*Salix*) stems make a good alternative to dogwood and will look just as striking with the eucalpytus leaves.

3 Once the full wreath shape is complete, twist short lengths of wire, approximately 3in (8cm) apart, around the branches to hold the wreath shape. Twist the ends of each length of wire together several times, and trim with scissors or small pliers.

4 Thread a piece of narrow green wire, approximately 8in (20cm) in length, around the base of a pine cone, making sure the wire is securely tucked into the ridges of the cone. Repeat for all of the pine cones.

5 Use the wire to attach the pine cone to the wreath, twisting the ends of the wire together several times to fix it in place. Attach the rest of the pine cones around the wreath in the same way.

6 Cut pieces of eucalyptus branch, approximately 12in (30cm) in length, and tuck them in between the dogwood twigs to hold them in position, taking care not to damage the leaves.

7 Continue to tuck the eucalyptus branches between the twigs until you have completed the whole wreath. Tie the ribbon in a bow at the top of the wreath and tuck the rosemary sprigs in at the top, behind the bow.

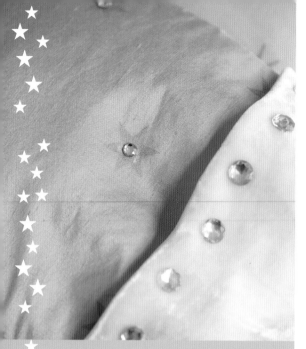

Starry silk and velvet stockings

These glamorous silk stockings feature a simple stamped star motif and sumptuous velvet cuffs finished with diamanté trims and thick tassels. They look beautiful hanging in a neat line from a mantelpiece.

Materials

Scissors

20in (50cm) silk, 54in (137cm) wide, per stocking

Pins and sewing needle

16in (40cm) cotton batting (wadding), for the lining

Star-shaped rubber stamp

Silver stamping ink

Sewing machine and matching thread

20in (50cm) silk velvet, 54in (137cm) wide, for the cuff

Fabric glue

Small and medium-sized diamanté shapes (for the stars and cuff)

Tassel with a hanging loop

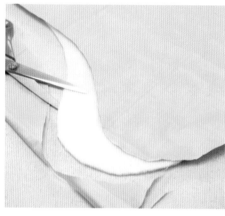

1 Using the template on page 121, enlarge the stocking pattern as directed and cut out the shape with scissors. Fold the silk fabric in half and pin the stocking pattern to the fabric to make a front and back. Cut through the two layers of fabric. Use the template again to cut out another stocking shape from the cotton batting (wadding).

2 Press the star stamp into the silver ink and stamp stars over one side of the stocking fabric, spaced approximately 2in (5cm) apart. Repeat on the other side of the stocking fabric if required. Allow the ink to dry completely.

3 With right sides of the silk fabric facing, pin the two stocking sections on top of the piece of cotton batting. Use the sewing machine with a matching thread to stitch through the three layers of fabric, leaving the top straight section of the stocking open. Trim and notch the curved edges of the fabric using the scissors.

4 Fold the silk velvet fabric in half lengthwise with the right sides facing. Pin and tack along the sides of the fabric and stitch together using the sewing machine. Turn to the right side.

5 Fold the velvet fabric in half with the velvet side facing the outside. Pin the fabric to the top of the silk stocking and handstitch in place using small whipstitches. Turn the stocking right side out and fold the velvet cuff over the top of the stocking, keeping it in place with a few stitches.

6 Use the glue to stick a small diamanté decoration carefully to the center of each printed star on the stocking. Leave the glue to dry thoroughly.

7 Use the glue to stick the larger diamanté decorations, approximately ¾in (2cm) apart, around the bottom of the cuff. Leave to dry completely.

8 Handstitch the tassel with the loop to the top of the stocking to finish before hanging up your stocking.

Top tip

The soft pastel colors of these silk stockings make them perfect for enhancing a subtle decorative scheme at Christmas. If you would like to make similar stockings for children, then simply opt for bolder and brighter fabrics, and increase the dimensions so they can be filled with lots of gifts.

Advent gift buckets

A simple and quirky alternative to the traditional Advent calender, these tiny metal buckets are decorated with a sweet heart motif and then filled with small, foil-wrapped chocolates and candy canes. The cute little buckets are finished off with a small numbered peg to denote the passing days of Advent.

Materials

Tracing paper and pencil

Piece of clear plastic (for the stencil)

Scalpel or sharp blade (for cutting out the stencil)

24 small metal buckets, approximately 2in (5cm) high

Masking tape (optional)

Green and red acrylic paint

Stencil brush

Scissors

Narrow ribbon or ric rac braid, approximately ½in (1cm) wide

Hot glue gun (or all-purpose glue)

Red gingham and polka-dot tissue paper

Foil-wrapped chocolates and candy canes

Numbered pegs

1 Using the template on page 124, trace the heart motif onto the paper with the pencil. Lay the piece of plastic on top of the template and carefully cut out the shape with a sharp blade or scalpel. Lay the stencil over the front of the bucket—you may wish to use small pieces of masking tape to hold it in position while you paint. Apply the paint carefully so that it does not bleed behind the stencil outline.

2 When the paint is completely dry, carefully peel off the stencil and repeat the process on the other buckets. I used both green and red paint to decorate the buckets with a heart motif.

3 Cut a length of ribbon or braid to fit around the bottom of the bucket, adding about ¼in (5mm) for overlap. Use glue or a hot glue gun to fix the ribbon in place, starting at the back of the bucket to hide the ribbon's raw edges. Repeat on the remaining buckets, using either ribbon or braid.

4 Cut a small square of tissue paper, measuring approximately 5 x 5in (13 x 13cm). Place the tissue paper in the bucket, folding in the edges neatly. Fill with chocolates and candy canes. Clip a numbered peg to the front of each bucket to finish. (If you can't buy numbered pegs, simply glue card motifs to pegs and add the numbers.)

Chapter Two
Table Settings

Cool & contemporary

Top tips

Cut the ends of the pompoms into other shapes, such as soft semi-circle to make each one slightly different.

Be candle aware—keep your pompom flowers a safe distance from any lit candles.

Materials

6 sheets of white tissue paper

Approximately 8in (20cm) strong ribbon per pompom

Pencil

Scissors

Piece of sheer ribbon (for hanging up each pompom)

Paper pompoms

These simple but effective, large paper flowers are made using sheets of folded tissue paper. They look great hung in groups above a festive table.

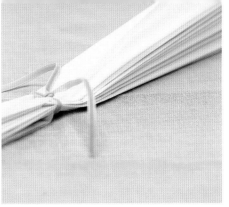

1 Lay a sheet of tissue paper flat on a table and begin folding the paper along the shorter edge in a concertina-style, making each fold about 1in (2.5cm) wide. Continue folding until the sheet is pleated and you have a long narrow length of folded tissue paper. Repeat for the other sheets of paper.

2 Carefully fold the paper in half lengthwise and make a fold to indicate the center. Tie the short-length ribbon around this point and secure tightly with several knots. You can tie the ends of the sheer ribbon on at this stage as well, which will make it easier to hang the pompom flower.

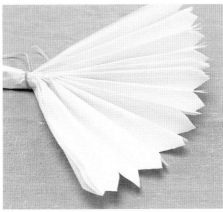

3 Using the pencil draw a triangle shape at both ends of the folded tissue paper. Cut out the pointed shape with the scissors at one end of the tissue paper and repeat at the other end. You will probably need very sharp scissors in order to cut through all of the layers of tissue paper.

4 Fan out the paper folds at one end, doing this as carefully as possible to avoid tearing the delicate tissue paper.

5 Gently unfold the pleats of tissue paper and coax them into a flower. This needs to be done gently as it is easy to tear the paper. Push your hand carefully inside the layers of tissue paper to separate them and create the fluffy shape. Repeat for the other side of the flower. Hang your pompoms in clusters above the table using the sheer ribbon.

Materials

8in (20cm) silver wire, $1/32$in (0.8mm) in diameter, per heart

Glass rocaille beads

Pliers (optional)

Silver ribbon

Scissors

Pretty beaded hearts

These delicate beaded hearts can be made in different sizes to decorate a Christmas tree, beautifully wrapped gifts, or simple linen napkins for the festive table, which are shown here. Tiny glass rocaille beads are threaded onto silver wire to create the heart shape. The hearts are easy for children to make, too, so ask them to help you create a festive collection.

1 Take an 8in (20cm) length of silver wire. Fold the wire in half and then carefully bend it into a V-shape to form the bottom of the heart.

2 Thread the beads onto both ends of the wire and continue threading until all of the wire is covered, leaving about 2in (5cm) bare at each end to form the hanging loop. Hold the wire ends and bend them inward to create the curved top of the heart. Twist the ends together to prevent the beads falling off the wire.

3 Twist the wire ends around the top of the heart and then twist the top ends of the wire together so they form a loop for hanging. You may find it easier to use pliers to do this if the wire is very strong. If you are making the hearts to decorate napkins, tie the ribbon around the napkin and thread the beaded heart onto one length of the ribbon. Finish tying the bow to fix the heart in position. Use scissors to trim the ribbon ends diagonally to prevent fraying.

Silver wreath centerpiece

For this centerpiece I used a ready-made wreath and decorated it with a selection of silver-sprayed pine cones and white hydrangea flowers. Filled with chunky pillar candles, this decorative wreath makes a stunning centerpiece for any festive dining table.

Materials

Scissors

1 white artificial hydrangea flowerhead

Medium and small natural pine cones
(approximately 10 medium cones
and enough small cones to fit
around the base of the wreath)

Silver spray paint

Shallow box (such as an old shoe box)

Ready-made silver or white
door wreath

Hot glue gun (or strong
all-purpose glue)

3 pillar candles

1 Use the scissors to cut some smaller hydrangea flowers from the bloom. You will need to cut four or five of these for the wreath.

2 Spray the pine cones with the silver spray paint. It is advisable to do this outside and wearing a mask to protect yourself from the fumes. Turn the pine cones over to ensure that all of the sides are covered with the silver paint. You'll need to apply a few coats of paint, so put the cones in a shallow box so that they can dry between coats.

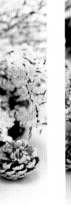

3 Glue the smaller silver pine cones close together to the base of the wreath. You may find it easier to use a hot glue gun for this if you have one because it will speed up the process.

4 Glue four or five hydrangea flowers to the top of the wreath, making sure they are evenly spaced. Glue the larger silver pine cones between the hydrangea flowers on top of the wreath. Fill the space inside the wreath with large pillar candles to finish.

Chandelier drop decorations

These sparkling glass decorations—suspended like delicate ice crystals—are made from chandelier drops, which are easy to find online. Quite often, a chandelier bought as a room light will come with spare drops, which you can then use to make these decorations. Hanging from sheer silver ribbon, they look stunning on a Christmas tree or tied to a special gift.

Materials

Selection of chandelier drops

Chandelier beads (with a hole at the top and bottom)

Silver ring hooks, ½in (1cm) in diameter, for threading

Pliers (optional)

5in (13cm) sheer ribbon, ½in (10mm) wide, per decoration

Scissors

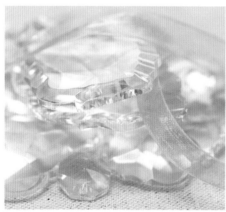

1 You can find beautiful chandelier drops and beads in many different sizes on the Internet from either auction websites or chandelier specialists. Many sell a selection of both new and vintage designs. They come in a host of shapes and sizes, but bear in mind that larger ones will be quite heavy when hanging from your Christmas tree.

2 Open out the first silver ring hook and push the end through the hole at the top of a chandelier drop. You may find it easier to use pliers to do this, as the ends of the wire can be quite sharp and tend to spring back into shape.

3 Thread the ring hook attached to the drop onto one end of a chandelier bead and then thread another ring hook onto the bead. Repeat until you have two chandelier beads sitting above the drop. Thread a final ring hook to the top bead so that you can thread through a ribbon to make a hanging loop.

4 Thread the ribbon through the top ring hook and tie a knot to form a hanging loop. Using scissors, cut the ends of the ribbon diagonally to stop the ends fraying.

Materials

Wooden labels

Silver acrylic paint

Paintbrush

Small silver gift boxes with handles (flat-packed for assembly at home)

Tissue paper

Scissors

Chocolates (or other tiny gifts)

Fine black pen

Narrow sheer ribbon, ¼in (5mm) wide, for attaching the label

1 white artificial hydrangea flowerhead

Hot glue gun (or all-purpose glue)

Silver box place holders

These ready-made gift boxes can be used to create the perfect place setting and a seasonal gift for your Christmas guests all in one. Simply fill each box with a handful of deliciously decadent chocolates and then decorate the top by adding some pretty artificial flowers and a tiny wooden name label inscribed with your guests' initials or full name.

1 Paint the wooden labels on both sides with silver paint and allow them to dry completely. (You could use silver spray paint if you are making a lot of boxes, in order to save time.)

2 Assemble the gift boxes and line them with a couple of sheets of tissue paper cut down to fit. Add the chocolates (or a special gift of your choice) and fold the boxes closed. Use the fine black pen to write the initials or name of each of your guests on the labels, thread the ribbon onto the labels, and tie them to the handles of the boxes.

3 Tuck a couple of artificial flowers pulled from the hydrangea flowerhead under the handle of each box or glue them in place on top of the box.

Silver crackers

You can easily make your own Christmas crackers using cardboard rolls and wrapping paper, and then decorate them to match the theme of your Christmas dining table. Adorned with lovely ribbons and crystal decorations, they really do make a stunning addition to any festive table and are sure to impress your guests. A gold variation of these crackers is shown on page 63.

1 Lay the sheet of wrapping paper flat on a table and fold one of the shorter edges of the paper over by 4¼in (11cm) toward the center of the paper. Repeat for the other short side of the paper.

2 Using the ruler and pencil, mark out a series of lines, approximately ⅝in (15mm) apart, along the folded edges of the paper. Then use the scissors to cut into each mark by approximately ¾in (2cm).

Materials

Sheet of wrapping paper, 14 x 7in (35 x 18cm), for each cracker

Ruler and pencil

Scissors

2 cardboard rolls, 3¼in (8.5cm) in length and 2in (5cm) in diameter

1 cardboard roll, 4in (10cm) in length and 2in (5cm) in diameter

Hot glue gun (or all-purpose glue)

Piece of cracker snap (for each cracker)

Gifts or candies (to fill the crackers)

Length of ribbon, 7in (18cm) long and 1½in (35mm) wide

Approximately 39in (1m) ribbon, ⅝in (15mm) wide, for the band and ribbon bows

2 wire beaded picks (crystal beads on wire)

1 small wooden glitter decoration (for the front of cracker)

Top tip

If you don't have time to make these Christmas crackers from scratch, then simply use wrapping paper and ribbons to cover ready-made crackers and pop some extra gifts inside for your guests!

3 Flatten out the paper, then lay the larger roll in the central section and the two shorter rolls in each end section so that the rolls are in line and parallel with the long sides of the paper. Roll the paper around the rolls and stick into place using glue or a hot glue gun. Insert a piece of cracker snap long enough to run through all three cracker sections. Add the small gift or candy to the central section. Wrap the wider ribbon around the center of the cracker, making sure the raw ends are at the back where the edges of the paper have been stuck down. Stick the ribbon securely with glue and allow to dry.

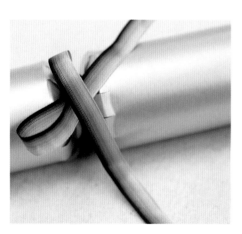

4 Tie a length of narrow ribbon around the cracker where you have cut the slits—do this carefully to avoid tearing the paper. Repeat at the other end of the cracker. Use the scissors to trim the ends of the ribbons diagonally to prevent them fraying.

5 Wind a wire beaded pick around the cracker on top of the narrower ribbon and twist the ends together to keep them in place. Trim the ends of the wire with the scissors if required. Repeat at the other end of the cracker.

6 Neatly glue another length of narrow ribbon over the wide ribbon in the center of the cracker and allow to dry. Stick a wooden glitter decoration on top of the ribbon to finish.

Traditional country

Materials

Scissors

Lengths of ribbon, ⅝in (15mm) wide
(you'll need enough for two rows
around the base of the pot)

3 small terracotta flowerpots

Hot glue gun (or all-purpose glue)

Ric rac braid (enough for two rows
around the rim of the pot)

3 small wooden hearts

Pillar candle (to fit the flowerpot)

Small stones

Real and/or artificial ivy leaves

Strung pine cones or similar (for the
base of the pot)

Terracotta pot centerpiece

Bring a little of the outdoors inside at Christmas with these charming, rustic-style terracotta pots. They are simply decorated with rows of ribbon and ric rac braid and then filled with ivy leaves and a pillar candle to create an effective and unusual table centerpiece. If you can't get hold of real ivy leaves, you can use artificial ones instead. Adding a string of tiny pine cones gives the centerpiece a final finishing touch.

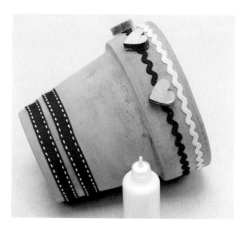

1 Cut two lengths of the ribbon to fit around the base of the flowerpot. Glue the first row of ribbon about ½in (1cm) from the base of the pot. Glue the second row of ribbon approximately ½in (1cm) above the first one, and leave the glue to dry completely.

2 Cut two lengths of ric rac braid to fit around the top of the pot. Stick the first row of ric rac braid approximately ⅝in (15mm) from the rim of the pot. Apply the second row of braid in the same way about ⅝in (15mm) below the first row. Allow the braid to dry.

3 Stick the wooden hearts, about 1¼in (3cm) apart, to the front of the flowerpot along the second row of ric rac braid, and leave the glue to dry. You may find it easier to use a hot glue gun to do this if you have one.

4 Place the pillar candle inside the flowerpot. You could fill around the candle with some small stones to keep it in position. Arrange the ivy leaves around the candle in layers. I used a combination of fresh and artificial ivy leaves here.

5 Cut the strung pine cones to fit around the base of the flowerpot and then tie the ends together. Alternatively, you can twist the ends together with a short length of wire.

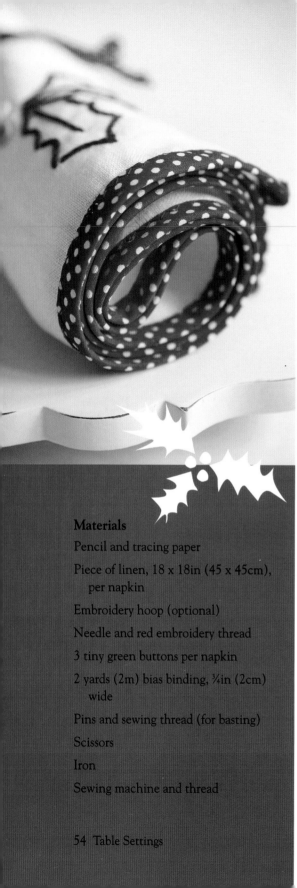

Embroidered napkins

These striking napkins can be used year after year for your Christmas festivities. Made in bold red and white linen, they feature a delicate embroidered holly motif and a border of patterned bias binding.

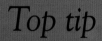

Top tip

To save time you could simply embroider the holly motif with tiny buttons on a ready-made napkin

Materials

Pencil and tracing paper

Piece of linen, 18 x 18in (45 x 45cm), per napkin

Embroidery hoop (optional)

Needle and red embroidery thread

3 tiny green buttons per napkin

2 yards (2m) bias binding, ¾in (2cm) wide

Pins and sewing thread (for basting)

Scissors

Iron

Sewing machine and thread

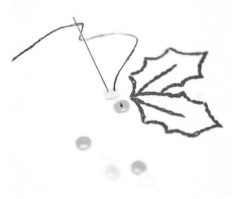

1 Using the template on page 124, trace the holly leaf motif onto the piece of paper with the pencil. Transfer the design to one corner of the napkin, securing this in the embroidery hoop, if you are using one, to keep the fabric taut. Work the motif using chain stitch in three strands of red embroidery thread.

2 Use the same thread to sew the three tiny buttons above the embroidered holly motif to depict the holly berries.

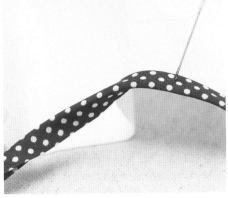

3 Carefully fold the bias binding in half lengthwise and use a hot iron to press it in place. Sandwich the edges of the napkin between the two layers of bias binding and baste into position, folding the corners carefully as you go. Fold the raw ends of the bias binding to the inside to prevent them fraying.

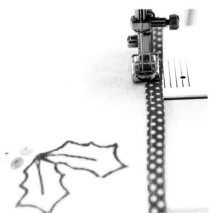

4 Use the sewing machine to topstitch the bias binding in place—you could use either a very narrow zigzag stitch or a simple straight stitch to sew over the edges of the bias binding. Remove the basting stitches.

Materials

Scissors

Piece of red linen fabric,
   17 x 14in (43 x 35cm),
   for each mat

Sharp needle

Pins and sewing thread
   (for basting)

63in (1.6m) gingham ribbon,
   ½in (10mm) wide

Sewing machine

Pencil and piece of thick paper

Sharp blade

Masking tape

Stencil brush

White fabric paint

6 red buttons, ⅝in (15mm)
   in diameter, for each mat

White embroidery thread

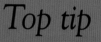

Top tip

If you are using a fabric
that has a loose weave, you
may wish to stitch the top
of the frayed edges using
a sewing machine in order
to stop them from fraying
any further.

Fringed tablemat

Stenciled with simple white stars, these linen tablemats feature fringed edges and pretty, red gingham ribbon borders to complement the embroidered napkins. Adding a red button to the center of each star gives a final decorative flourish.

1 Use the scissors to cut out a tablemat from the linen fabric according to the dimensions given in the Materials list. Lay the piece of fabric on a flat surface and use the sharp needle to pull the threads gently away from the fabric to create the fringed edging. This is quite a lengthy process and requires patience, particularly if the fabric has a tight weave. Repeat on all sides of the fabric so that each fringed edge measures around ½in (1cm) in depth.

2 Pin and tack the gingham ribbon around the edges of the tablemat, approximately 1½in (4cm) from the fringed edge. Topstitch along both edges of the ribbon using the sewing machine. Remove the tacking stitches.

3 Using the template on page 124, trace the star-shaped motif onto the piece of thick paper. Use the sharp blade to cut out the design carefully. Place the stencil on the tablemat along the shorter edge so that the stenciled motifs will run down the sides of the mat. Use small pieces of masking tape to fix the stencil onto the fabric and fill in the star with the stencil brush and white fabric paint. Repeat on the other side of the mat and allow the paint to dry.

4 Once the fabric paint is completely dry, sew a red button in the center of each star using the embroidery thread.

Golden & glamorous

Gold and pink Christmas cake

Instead of the traditional Christmas pudding, why not create a stunning and edible decorative centerpiece for your dining table? This striking cake is made by layering Christmas fruit cakes and then covering them with delicious fondant icing decorated with edible golden shimmer and the softest pink velvet ribbons.

Top tip

You can save time by buying fruit cakes and then icing them yourself before decorating. Most stores sell plain cakes in various sizes for the festive season. You could opt for sponge cake instead of fruit if you wish.

1 Roll out the fondant icing and cover the cakes, trimming the edges neatly so that they sit smoothly around the sides of the cakes. Use a sharp knife to trim off the bulkier bits of icing around the edges. Roll out more of the fondant icing until it is approximately ¼–½in (8–10mm) thick and cut out some star shapes using the different sized cutters.

2 Make the star decoration by layering the star shapes together with the largest one at the bottom. Use a blob of icing between each star to stick them to each other. Apply the edible gold shimmer to the star decoration with the paintbrush. Also apply a layer of gold shimmer to the smaller cake.

3 Place the star decoration on top of the smaller cake and fix in place with a blob of icing. Wrap the sheer gold ribbon around the cake and fix into position at the back—you can do this using a hot glue gun or a sharp wooden cocktail stick. Wrap the pink velvet ribbon around the gold ribbon and fix in place.

Materials

White fondant icing (you can buy this ready-rolled if necessary)

Rolling pin

2 plain fruit cakes in two different sizes

Sharp knife

Star-shaped cutters in assorted sizes

Edible gold shimmer and paintbrush

Sheer gold ribbon, 1¼in (30mm wide), to fit around the cakes

Hot glue gun (or all-purpose glue)

Pale pink velvet ribbon (enough to fit around the cakes)

Diamanté decorations (for the ribbon)

4 Stick the diamanté decorations around the velvet ribbon. Place the gold cake on top of the white cake, and fix another layer of gold and pink ribbon around the larger cake. (I layered two cakestands with gold paper doilies and then filled the lower cakestand with golden baubles to finish.)

Sequinned cone place settings

These stunning place settings are made from polystyrene cones (available from craft stores) studded with beads and sequins. Top each cone with a painted golden star bearing your guests' initials to create a glamorous effect for a festive dining table.

Materials

Gold acrylic paint and paintbrush

Polystyrene cones

Wooden stars (for the tops of the trees)

Gold pearl beads

Dressmaker's pins

Gold and white cup sequins

Gimp pins (shorter pins for the cone top)

Single pin with beaded head for each cone

Fine black pen

Hot glue gun (or all-purpose glue)

1 Paint the polystyrene cones and the tree-top stars in gold and leave to dry thoroughly. You may need several coats of paint to achieve full coverage. This helps prevent any unsightly white gaps between the sequins.

2 Starting at the base of each cone, thread a pearl bead onto a dressmaker's pin followed by a cup sequin, and press the pin firmly into the cone. Repeat in neat rows around the cone, alternating two or three rows of gold sequins with a single row of white sequins until you reach the top of the cone. You'll find it easier to use the gimp pins at the top of the cone because they won't stick out on the other side when you press them in.

3 Push the single-beaded pin through the top of each cone and use this to support the gold stars. Write the initials of your guests on the star labels with the pen. Apply a dab of glue to hold the star in position at the top of each cone.

Golden glitter glass votives

You can use these festive glass votives to adorn your Christmas dining table or mantelpiece and bring a soothing ambience to your celebration. They are so simple to make, using plain glasses trimmed with decorative gold sequinned braid and featuring a glittering golden Christmas tree.

Materials

Pencil and tracing paper

Small glass or plain votive

Masking tape (optional)

White (PVA) glue

Fine paintbrush

Gold glitter

Teaspoon (optional)

3 small gold cup sequins per glass

Hot glue gun (or all-purpose glue)

Gold sequinned braid

1 Using the template on page 123, trace the Christmas tree motif onto the piece of paper with the pencil. Place the template inside the glass—you could use small pieces of masking tape to hold the template in place while you work. Fill in the tree shape on the outside of the glass using the glue and paintbrush.

Using the template on page 123

Top tip

You can, of course, ring in the seasonal changes by featuring different Christmas designs, such as holly leaves, chiming bells, or even snowmen. Choose different shades of glitter to match the decorative scheme of your festive table or room.

2 Carefully pour the gold glitter over the Christmas tree shape; you may find it helpful to use a teaspoon to do this. Shake off the excess glitter and repeat the process twice so that there are three tree motifs around the glass. Leave the glue to dry completely.

3 Glue a small gold cup sequin to the base of the Christmas trees on each glass. You may find it easier to use a hot glue gun do this.

4 Cut a length of gold sequinned braid to fit around the rim of each glass. Carefully stick the braid to the rim of the glass—using the hot glue gun if you have one—and leave to dry thoroughly.

Gold sequinned table runner

This sumptuous table runner, which is made from gold and bronze voile fabric, will add a touch of glamour to any Christmas table. You can make the runner to fit the length of your dining table or, alternatively, make two or three shorter runners that can then be laid across the width of your table. Either way, this runner is guaranteed to impress your guests and turn your festive celebration—or any special occasion—into something truly memorable.

Materials

Bronze voile fabric, 22in (55cm) wide by the length of your table

Gold voile fabric, 14in (35cm) wide by the length of your table

2 lengths of gold braid (to fit the length of your table)

39in (1m) gold beaded fringing

39in (1m) gold sequinned braid

Iron

Needle and thread (white and gold)

Sewing machine

Tape measure

Scissors

Pins

1 Lay the bronze voile flat on your work surface and fold the longer edges to the inside by 2in (5cm). Press flat using a warm iron. Lay the gold voile on top of the bronze voile, so that the raw edges meet and pin it into position.

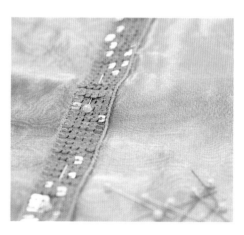

2 Lay the gold braid along the raw edges of the voile fabrics to cover them and then pin into place. Tack the braid to the fabrics with a needle and thread.

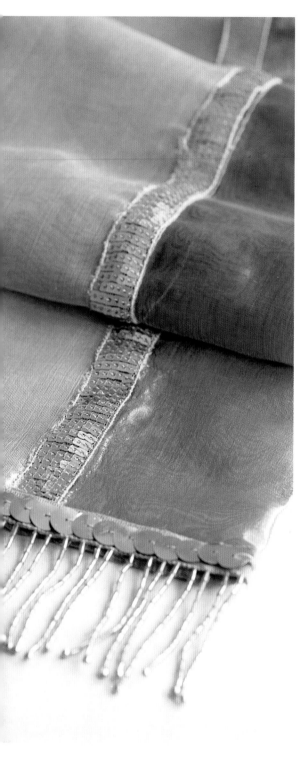

3 Use the sewing machine to topstitch the gold braid neatly into place along both long edges of the runner and remove the tacking stitches by hand.

4 Fold the hem of the fabric toward the inside by about ½in (1cm) at the top and bottom of the runner and tack into place. Lay the gold beaded fringing along these shorter edges and tack into position. Use the sewing machine to stitch the beaded fringing to the runner along both edges. Again, remove the tacking stitches.

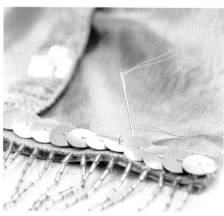

5 Handstitch the gold sequinned braid on top of the beaded fringing, using the holes in each sequin as the marker for sewing. Tuck the raw edges of the braid to the inside of the fabric to finish.

Top tip

If you wish, you could adapt these instructions to make a linen table runner to accompany the traditional country-style table setting featured on pages 50–51. Use a length of linen fabric and replace the sequin trim and fringing with ribbon or braid and miniature pompoms.

Chapter Three
Cards, Giftwrap & Labels

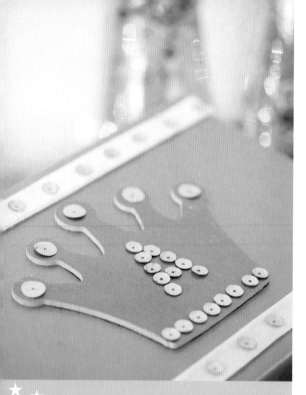

Velvet ribbon and gold wrapping with gift label

Warm gold and soft pink are a lovely color combination and make this stylish gift-wrapping idea look very special indeed. The matching wooden gift label is a perfect keepsake for the recipient and can be used in future as a Christmas decoration.

Materials

Gold wrapping paper

Sticky tape

Scissors

Pale pink velvet ribbon, ⅝in (15mm) wide

Hot glue gun (or all-purpose glue)

Small gold cup sequins

MDF crown motifs

Gold acrylic paint

Old plate

Paintbrush

5 flat gold sequins, ½in (1cm) in diameter

Pencil

1 Wrap your gift, making sure the edges and corners are folded neatly into place. (Use the scissors to trim the paper at both ends so that they fold in at the sides of the parcel and don't overlap the top or bottom.)

2 Cut two lengths of the pale pink velvet ribbon to fit around the gift and allow for ½in (1cm) of overlap. (You can run the ribbon around either the longer or shorter sides of the gift.) Glue the ribbons into place along both sides of the gift. You may find it easier to do this with a glue gun.

Top tip

If you wish, drill a small hole in the top of the crown and thread with a length of narrow sheer ribbon so that it can be used afterward as a Christmas tree decoration.

3 Glue the small gold cup sequins along the center of the ribbon, spacing them approximately ¾in (2cm) apart. Repeat for the second band of ribbon and leave to dry completely.

4 Pour a small amount of gold paint onto the plate and paint the MDF crown. You will probably need to apply two coats to ensure good coverage. Allow the paint to dry thoroughly. (If you can't find MDF crown shapes in your craft store, you could cut a similar shape from thick cardboard.)

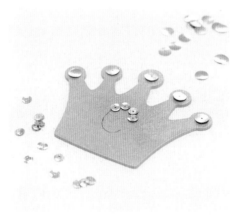

5 Glue the larger gold sequins onto the top of the crown in the center of each prong. Leave the glue to dry.

6 Draw the recipient's initial on the crown using the pencil. Stick more of the smaller gold cup sequins along the line forming the initial.

7 Glue a row of the smaller gold cup sequins along the bottom straight edge of the crown, approximately ¼in (5mm) apart. Stick the crown to the front of the gift to finish.

Handstitched label

These cute gift tags for attaching to presents are made from standard parcel labels and decorated with red buttons and rows of embroidered running stitch. They make the perfect gift label to go with the ric rac gift wrap on page 79—even utilitarian items are put to good use at Christmas!

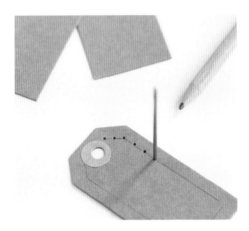

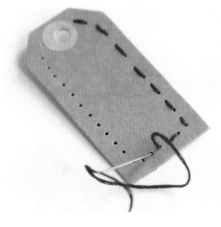

1 Use the ruler and pencil to draw a soft line, about ⅛in (3mm) from the edge, all around the brown parcel label. Place the label on the foam board and use the large needle to pierce holes along the pencil lines, spaced approximately ¼in (5mm) apart. These will form the stitching holes for the embroidery. Rub out the pencil lines using the eraser.

2 Thread the needle with the red embroidery thread and work a row of running stitches around the edges of the parcel label.

3 Glue two buttons to the center of the label. You may find it easier to use a hot glue gun to do this. It is better to glue the buttons rather than sew them on, as you won't be able to write on the back of the label if the buttons are sewn on.

4 Thread the ric rac braid through the hole at the top of the parcel label and tie securely. Thread the ends of the braid to your parcel to finish.

Ric rac gift wrap

This simple yet effective gift wrap uses plain brown parcel paper and lengths of red and natural ric rac braid glued in bands around the gift. This striking homemade wrapping is beautifully finished off with a matching, handstitched gift tag.

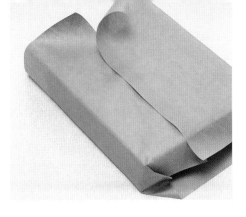

1 Wrap your gift, making sure that the edges and corners are folded neatly into place. (Use the scissors to trim the paper at both ends so that they fold in at the sides of the parcel and don't overlap the top or bottom.)

2 Cut lengths of ric rac to fit around the whole present, allowing an extra ½in (1cm) for overlap. Glue the ric rac to the back of the gift: start with a band of narrow ric rac, then two bands of wider ric rac, and then another narrow band, with each band spaced approximately ⅝in (15mm) apart. You may find it easier to do this with a glue gun if you have one. Repeat on the opposite side of the gift.

Materials

Sheet of brown parcel paper

Sticky tape

Scissors

Lengths of red and natural-colored ric rac braid in both a narrow and wider width (enough to fit the size of your gift)

Hot glue gun (or all-purpose glue)

3 Next cut two lengths of narrow, natural-colored ric rac, lay them at right angles to the first bands of ric rac, and tuck them under one of the bands. Glue the two lengths of ric rac to the back of the parcel, as before, using strong glue or a hot glue gun if you prefer.

4 Write the name of the lucky recipient on the handstitched gift label and tie the label with a knot or bow to one of the rows of ric rac.

Felt pouches

These cute felt pouches are the perfect size for holding gift vouchers, which you may be giving as Christmas presents. They make a charming alternative to a plain white envelope and are a lovely personal touch. Decorated with ribbon, ric rac braid, and buttons, they are finished with simple blanket-stitched edges.

Materials

Pencil and paper

Scissors

Pins

1 sheet colored felt (a sheet of 8 x 12in/ A4-sized felt will make two pouches)

Embroidery needle

Ribbon and ric rac braid (to fit the pouch) and thread to match

Embroidery thread in a color to contrast with the felt

Selection of buttons and beads

Hot glue gun (or all-purpose glue)

Decorative pins (optional)

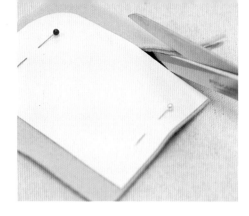

1 Trace the pouch pattern from the template on page 124 onto the piece of paper using the pencil. Cut out the pattern for the pouch with the scissors. Pin the pattern to two layers of the felt and then cut out the pouch shape.

2 Sew the ribbon and ric rac braid by hand to the top and bottom of the front piece of pouch. Use tiny running stitches, making sure they are spaced approximately ⅝in (1.5cm) from the top and bottom edges.

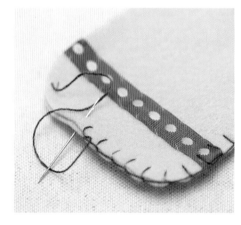

3 Place the two pieces of felt together, wrong sides facing, and work blanket stitch around the edges, leaving the top straight edge of the pouch open. When you have finished stitching the two sections together, work more blanket stitch around the two open edges at the top of the pouch.

4 To finish, decorate the pouch with a selection of buttons and beads. Simply stitch the buttons on by hand and use glue to attach the beads. If you wish, close the pouch with a decorative pin.

Materials

- Piece of tracing paper, 6 x 6in (15 x 15cm)
- Pencil
- Square blank card, approximately 6 x 6in (15 x 15cm)
- Foam board (for piercing and stitching the holes)
- Masking tape
- Large needle
- Thimble (optional)
- Embroidery needle
- Ivory-colored embroidery thread
- Scissors
- 8 miniature buttons, ¼in (5mm) in diameter
- Hot glue gun (or all-purpose glue)
- Miniature velvet bow (or 4in/10cm of narrow velvet ribbon to make one)

Embroidered snowflake card

This unusual embroidered snowflake card is, in fact, very easy to make and involves sewing a simple backstitch through punched holes. Finished with miniature buttons and a tiny velvet bow, it truly is a keepsake card.

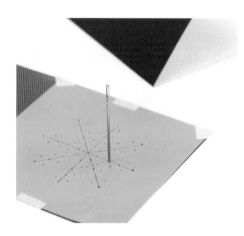 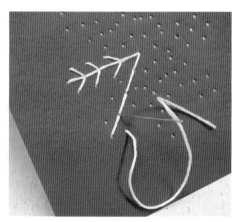

1 Trace the snowflake design from the template on page 123 onto the square sheet of tracing paper using the pencil. Lay the card out flat on the foam board and stick the tracing paper on top using small pieces of masking tape around the edges. Insert the large needle through each dot shown on the template to mark out the snowflake design. You may find it easier to use a thimble for this to protect your fingers.

2 Thread the embroidery needle with the embroidery thread and insert the needle from the back of the card to the front. Begin to work backstitch along the holes pierced in the card. You will see the snowflake design begin to appear as you embroider.

3 When the embroidery is finished, cast off and place the card flat on the table. Stick the eight miniature buttons at the end of each point of the snowflake and allow the glue to dry completely. You may find this quicker with a hot glue gun if you have one.

4 Make a tiny bow from narrow velvet ribbon, or use a ready-made bow, and stick it to the center of the embroidered snowflake design to finish.

Top tip

If you are short of time during the busy festive season, try piercing two cards together, one on top of the other, with the large needle. Use small pieces of masking tape to prevent the cards from slipping around while you pierce them.

Glitter tree card

Simple yet effective, these cards are stenciled with glittery tree shapes. They are great cards to make in bulk for friends and family—just buy large pots of glitter in different colors. If you are making lots of cards, cut out the stencil in a piece of plastic because paper will get too wet when used repeatedly. However, it is much more difficult to cut plastic with a craft knife, so do this very carefully.

Materials

Paper and pencil

Sharp craft knife

Blank cards and envelopes

White (PVA) glue

Stencil brush

Glitter in a contrasting color

Diamanté decorations

Hot glue gun (or all-purpose glue)

1 Trace the tree motif from the template on page 124 onto the piece of paper using the pencil. Carefully cut out the tree motif with the sharp craft knife. Place the tree stencil in the center of the blank card and apply a layer of white glue using the stencil brush.

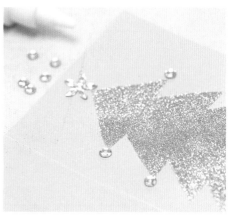

2 Pour the glitter liberally onto the stencil and leave for about 10 minutes so that the glue begins to dry. Shake off any excess glitter.

3 When the glue is completely dry, carefully lift away the stencil motif to reveal the glittery tree motif.

4 Finish the tree with tiny diamanté decorations. (You could use a hot glue gun to do this if you have one.)

Fun button snowman card

You can use a selection of different sized buttons to create this cute Christmas card which depicts a festive snowman. Add arms and a hat brim made from pipecleaners and a felt nose, plus lots of sparkly glitter to represent snow. Alternatively, you can use red and white buttons and pipecleaners to make a Santa Claus card instead.

Materials

Piece of blank card

Foam board (for piercing and stitching the holes)

3 white buttons (small, medium, and large)

Large needle (to make holes for sewing)

White embroidery thread

Embroidery needle

Scissors

All-purpose glue

Black pipecleaner

Scraps of orange and black felt, for the hat and nose

Paintbrush

White glitter

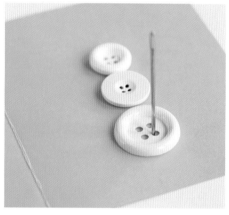

1 Place the piece of card on the foam board and then lay the three buttons in descending order in a column on the card. Carefully pierce each hole in the buttons with the large needle so it goes through the card. This makes it easier to sew on the buttons without bending the card.

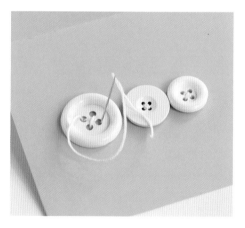

2 Sew the buttons to the card using the white embroidery thread and needle. Cast off your sewing and trim off the ends of the thread. You may wish to put a tiny blob of glue on the inside of the card over the thread ends to secure them in place.

3 Cut two arms, approximately 1in (2.5cm) long, and a brim for the snowman's hat, measuring around ¾in (2cm), from the pipecleaner. Glue these to the card in their correct positions.

4 Cut a small oblong, measuring ½in (1cm) by ⅝in (15mm), from the black felt and glue it to the card to finish the hat. Cut a tiny triangle for the snowman's nose from the orange felt and glue it to the top button. Leave to dry thoroughly. Apply small blobs of glue over the card using the paintbrush and shake the glitter over the blobs for the snowflakes. Pour off excess glitter and leave to dry.

Chapter Four
Edible Gifts

Chocolate truffles

These delicious truffles are so simple to make—and children will love helping you make them, too. I added a coating of royal icing, edible holly leaves, and a rolled fondant berry to make the truffles look like tiny Christmas puddings. If you don't have time to make a chocolate sponge cake, then use some ready-made muffins or cupcakes instead. This recipe will make around 8 truffles.

Materials

7oz (200g) semi-sweet (dark) chocolate

Approximately one-third of a chocolate sponge cake (or 2 ready-made chocolate muffins or cupcakes) to make 2 cups sponge cake crumbs

⅜ cup (75g) ground almonds

Cocoa powder

Royal icing, made using confectioner's (icing) sugar mixed with water

Green and red rolled fondant (you can use ready-to-use fondant)

Mixing bowl

Saucepan

Plastic wrap (clingfilm)

Rolling pin

Holly leaf cutter

1 Break the chocolate into small pieces and place in the mixing bowl over a pan of simmering water (you can also melt the chocolate in a microwave if you prefer). Remove the pan from the heat once the chocolate has melted. Use your fingers to crumble up the chocolate sponge cake and add it to the mixing bowl along with the ground almonds. Place in the refrigerator for about an hour, covering the bowl with some plastic wrap (clingfilm).

2 Take about a dessert spoon of mixture and roll it between the palms of your hands to form a ball shape. Sprinkle some cocoa powder onto a plate and roll the ball in the cocoa powder, making sure it is completely covered. Shake off any excess cocoa powder. Repeat for the other truffles.

3 Make up a bowl of royal icing with the confectioner's (icing) sugar and a small amount of water, following the directions on the sugar packet. Gently pour about a teaspoon of icing over the top of the truffle and allow it to dribble down the sides. Leave the icing to dry completely.

4 Using the rolling pin, roll out the green rolled fondant and cut out the holly leaf shapes with the cutter. Roll a small ball of red rolled fondant to make a berry for the top of each truffle. Use a small amount of royal icing to stick the holly leaves to the top of the truffle and finish off with a red berry.

Materials

6 tablespoons (75g) unsalted butter

½ cup (115g) superfine (caster) sugar

1 extra large (large) egg

1½ cups (200g) all-purpose (plain) flour

½ teaspoon baking powder

½ teaspoon salt

Tubes of ready-made colored icing

Plastic wrap (clingfilm)

Rolling pin

Cookie cutters in different shapes

Plastic drinking straw

Baking sheet

Wire rack

Wax (greaseproof) paper

8in (20cm) ribbon or ric rac braid
   per cookie

Cookie tree decorations

These delicious festive cookies are decorated with colorful icing and then strung with decorative ribbons to create edible tree decorations. The red, green, and white icing is applied neatly around the edges of the cookies, as well as in different patterns across the surface. Here, I have decorated the cookies with stars, stripes, and dots. This recipe will make approximately 18 cookies.

1 Preheat the oven to 350°F/180°C/gas 4. Cream the butter and sugar until soft, and then beat in the egg. Sift in the flour, baking powder, and salt. Roll the dough into a ball, wrap in plastic wrap (clingfilm), and put in the refrigerator for about an hour.

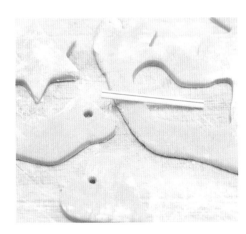

2 Roll out the cookie mixture to a thickness of approximately ½in (1cm) and use the cookie cutters to cut out the different shapes. Cut down the plastic drinking straw to a length of about 4in (10cm) using scissors and pierce the top of each cookie with it to make a hole for the ribbon.

3 Bake the cookies on a baking sheet lined with wax (greaseproof) paper for about 8–10 minutes or until golden brown. Remove the cookies from the oven and place them on a wire rack. Use the plastic drinking straw to repierce the holes if they have closed up during cooking. Leave the cookies to cool. Decorate each cookie with icing as desired.

4 Cut pieces of ribbon and ric rac braid, approximately 8in (20cm) long, and thread them through the holes in each cookie. Tie in a knot and trim the ribbon ends diagonally using scissors to stop them fraying.

Miniature Christmas cakes

If you always bake your own Christmas fruit cake, then why not make two of them and use one to create these sweet little Christmas cakes for your guests? Decorated with lengths of pretty, brightly colored ribbon, they also make lovely gifts for friends and family if you present them in a tiny box.

Materials

Homemade or store-bought fruit cake

White rolled fondant (use the ready-rolled version to save time if you prefer)

Royal icing, made using confectioner's (icing) sugar mixed with water

Sugar pearls (around 9 per cake)

Sugar flower decorations

Sharp knife

Rolling pin

Chopstick (to pierce the holes for the sugar pearls)

Approximately 5in (13cm) ribbon, ¾in (2cm) wide, per miniature cake

Cocktail sticks or sticky tape (to secure the ribbons)

1 Use a sharp knife to cut the fruit cake into tubular shapes, approximately 2in (5cm) wide by 3in (8cm) high. Press them in gently at the sides to smooth the edges in case the fruit in the cake creates any lumpy shapes.

2 Roll out the fondant with a rolling pin (unless you are using ready-rolled fondant), cut out a small circle with the knife, and drape it over the cake. Cut the edges and gently mold the ends of the fondant so that they fit the edges of the cake. You may need to make gentle pleats in the fondant and trim them again with the knife. Don't worry if the edges aren't neat, as they will be covered with ribbon.

3 Use the chopstick to pierce holes, about ½in (1cm) apart, around the top of each cake. This will help keep the sugar pearls in place. Make up a bowl of royal icing using confectioner's (icing) sugar and a small amount of water, following the directions on the packet. Put a blob of icing in each hole, press the pearl into place, and allow the icing to dry.

4 Wrap a ribbon around each cake, making sure the bottom of the ribbon sits at the base of the cake. Use a sharp cocktail stick or a piece of sticky tape to secure the ends of the ribbon. Use a little icing to stick a sugar flower to the middle of each cake. Remember to remove the stick before eating the cake!

Candied peel

These chocolate-covered orange pieces are easy to make and very delicious! Presented in a gold gift box and nestled among layers of pretty tissue paper, they would make a wonderful gift at any time of year, but are particularly welcome at Christmas. You can also tie the strips of peel together in little bundles with some sheer white ribbon.

1 Carefully cut the oranges into neat quarters on the chopping board using the sharp knife, and remove the flesh.

2 Cut the peel into strips, about ½in (12mm) wide, and then remove as much of the pith as possible with the knife. Try not to damage the peel of the orange as you cut the strips. Set aside on the chopping board.

3 Place the sugar and water in the saucepan, bring to a boil, and boil for 5 minutes. Add the orange-peel strips and simmer in the sugar-and-water mixture for about 2 hours, during which time the mixture should reduce significantly. Remove from the heat and allow to cool. Drain the peel and leave to cool on parchment paper. Sprinkle with a small amount of sugar if required.

Materials

4 large oranges

1¼ cups (275g) superfine (caster) sugar, plus extra for dusting

4 cups (1 litre) water

10½ oz (300g) good-quality semi-sweet (dark) chocolate, minimum 70% cocoa solids

Chopping board and a small sharp knife

Parchment paper

Bowl and a saucepan

4 Break the chocolate into small chunks and melt them in a bowl placed over a saucepan of simmering water, stirring occasionally to help break down the pieces quickly. Dip the orange peel strips in the chocolate so that they are about half covered. Return the strips to the parchment paper and leave to cool completely before serving or wrapping.

Homemade fudge

With its delicious texture, smooth creamy taste, and delicate color, fudge is a favorite with many people at any time of the year and not just at Christmas. I added whole blanched almonds to the recipe for a nutty flavor and topped the finished fudge with almonds as well. Wrapped in a cellophane bag tied with a pretty gold ribbon, this fudge would make a delightful Christmas gift.

Materials

14oz (400g) can condensed milk

⅔ cup (150ml) milk

2¼ cups (450g) light Demerara sugar

1 stick (125g) butter, plus extra for greasing

¼ cup (110g) blanched almonds, plus extra to decorate

Deep baking pan

Wax (greaseproof) paper

Saucepan

1 Line a deep baking pan, which is approximately 8in (20cm) square, with some wax (greaseproof) paper and lightly grease the bottom and sides.

2 Place all the ingredients apart from the almonds in the saucepan and heat gently until the sugar dissolves. Once the mixture comes to a boil, simmer for about 10 minutes, stirring all the time. (You will know that the mixture is sufficiently heated if a small amount poured into a bowl of cold water forms a soft ball.) Remove the pan from the heat and use a wooden spoon to beat the mixture vigorously for about 15 minutes. Fold the almonds into the mixture.

3 Gently pour the fudge mixure into the baking pan, making sure that it settles into the corners and that the almonds are spread evenly throughout the mixture.

4 After about half an hour and before the mixture has set, use a sharp knife to score the fudge without cutting all the way through.

5 Remove the fudge from the tray and press an almond into the center of each square. Cut the fudge into squares. If you are giving the fudge as a gift, put the pieces in a clear cellophane bag, tie with a sheer gold ribbon, and perhaps decorate with a pretty diamanté pick.

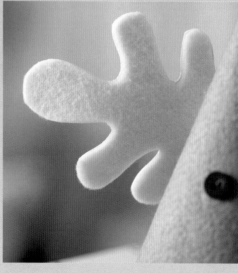

Chapter Five

For Children

Snow globes

These simple yet magical snow globes are made from jelly (jam) jars and decorated with snowflake designs. Filled with vintage-style Christmas cake decorations and a generous sprinkling of silver glitter, they would make a great gift for any child. Children will love to make these snow globes, too, although they will need some adult supervision.

Materials

Paper and pencil

Jelly (jam) jar with lid

Sticky tape

Three-dimensional fabric pen in white

Waterproof tile adhesive

Christmas tree decoration

2 cups (500ml) distilled water

2 teaspoons glycerine

1 teaspoon clear or pale-colored dish-washing detergent

Measuring jug

Silver glitter

Clear silicone bathroom sealant

1 Use the template on page 124 to trace the snowflake design using the pencil onto a small square of paper. Place the paper inside the jar and use some sticky tape in order to hold it in place. Carefully fill in the snowflake outline with tiny dots using the white three-dimensional fabric pen. Allow to dry for an hour or until completely dry.

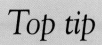

Top tip

You can create a collection of snow globes using jars in different sizes. As well as Christmas trees, try using other decorations, such as a Santa Claus or snowman. Adding colored glitter will also create striking effects.

2 Put a blob of the waterproof tile adhesive in the middle of the underside of the jar lid. Leave the adhesive to dry for an hour or so or until it has hardened slightly. Press the Christmas tree decoration into the adhesive and leave to dry completely.

3 Mix the distilled water, glycerine, and dish-washing detergent in the jug. Add about two teaspoons of glitter, and stir. Pour the mixture into the jar to the brim. Use the spoon to scoop off any bubbles that may be produced by the dish-washing detergent.

4 To make the jar extra watertight, use a small amount of clear silicone bathroom sealant around the top edge before tightly screwing on the lid.

Top tip

Make larger snowflakes and hang them by lengths of thread from a window to give the illusion of snow falling outside. These snowflakes also look great made in silver and gold paper if you want a little more sparkle!

Materials

4in (10cm) square thin white paper per snowflake

Pencil

Scissors

Sticky tack

60in (1.5m) green ric rac braid (for the bow)

Paper snowflakes

Paper snowflakes have many different uses and make a cheap and cheerful Christmas decoration—here they frame a pretty angel ornament. I used small snowflakes to create a pretty wreath shape which I finished with a green ric rac bow. Although white paper is an obvious choice for making snowflakes, you can also use colored paper to tie in with a decorative scheme or just to add some bold splashes of color at Christmas.

1 Fold the piece of paper in half diagonally and then in half again, also diagonally. Repeat this twice so that you have a piece of triangular-shaped paper.

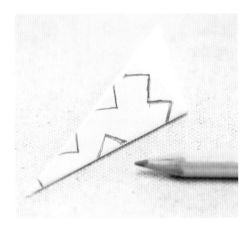

2 Use the pencil to draw triangles on the paper, putting two on one long side of the triangle and one on the other long side. Draw a zigzag shape of triangles along the top straight edge of the paper triangle and a small line at the other pointed end.

3 Trim the small line at the pointed end of the triangle first and then use the scissors to cut out all the triangular shapes you have drawn.

4 Unfold the paper very carefully to reveal the snowflake design. You will need a total of 12 paper snowflakes to create the wall wreath. When you have finished, use pieces of sticky tack to fix the wreath to the wall. Cut the length of ric rac braid in half and tie both lengths together into a bow. Stick the bow to the top of the wreath to finish.

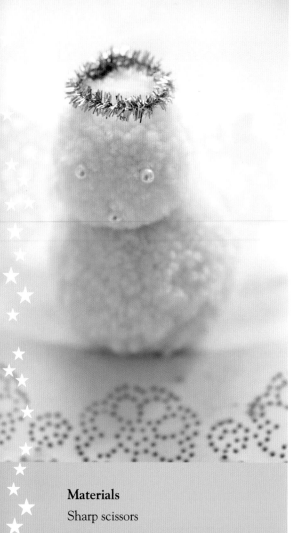

Pompom angels

These sweet little angels with their delicate paper-doily wings are a twist on the traditional woollen pompom. You can make them in soft pastel colors or perhaps all in white if you are looking for a pretty Christmas decoration for the tree or table. Topped with a little golden halo, they look utterly adorable.

Materials

Sharp scissors

Pale pink, blue, or white wool

2 discs of card (cardboard), measuring approximately 4in (10cm) in diameter, with a ¾in (2cm) hole in the center

Crochet hook (optional)

Small paper doily

Hot glue gun (or all-purpose glue)

3 small pearl beads (for the angel's eyes and mouth)

Gold chenille stem (pipecleaner) for the halo

1 Cut a length of wool, approximately 6½ft (2m) in length, and fold it in half. Thread the wool through the hole in the center of the two discs and tie a knot to keep it in place. Start to wind the wool around the discs, pushing it through the central hole each time. When you reach the end of the wool, cut another length and tie it to the end of the first length before continuing to wind the wool.

2 Continue winding the wool around the discs as tightly as you can. As the wool gets thicker, it will become more difficult to pull it through the hole and so you may wish to use a crochet hook or something similar to pull it through. Remember that the more wool you use, the fluffier your pompom will be.

3 When you have finished winding the wool, carefully cut the wool around the edges of the discs using sharp scissors. This will make the ends of the wool fray and begin to form the pompom shape.

4 After cutting the wool around the discs, take another length of wool, around 12in (30cm) long, and fold it in half. Pull it between the two discs, wrap it around a couple of times, and then tie it in a tight knot. This will keep the pompom together.

5 Carefully pull away the discs to reveal the pompom and use your fingers to fluff it into shape. Repeat the above process using two 3in (8cm) discs to make a smaller pompom for the angel's head. Use the loose wool ends of the two pompoms to tie them together, pull tightly, and knot the wool several times before trimming the ends with scissors. Fold the paper doily in half and cut with scissors. Fold each semi-circle in half again and glue them to the center back of the larger pompom.

6 Use glue to stick the pearl eyes and mouth to the front of the smaller pompom, which forms the angel's head.

7 Make a circular shape, approximately 1in (2.5cm) in diameter, with the gold chenille stem (pipecleaner). Twist the ends to secure them in place and trim them with scissors. Stick the halo to the top of the angel's head with glue—it may be easier to use a hot glue gun to do this if you have one.

Top tip

These pompoms can also be used to make other decorations. For example, try making a robin using brown and red wool, and add chenille-stem (pipecleaner) legs and a beak. Or, alternatively, make a cute snowman in white wool with a black felt hat and button eyes.

Felt cone reindeer

This is a fun Christmas decoration for children to make as you prepare for the festive season. This cute little reindeer is made from a cone of card covered with light brown felt and a pair of shapely antlers in cream-colored felt. The cone shape is versatile and can be used for many different homemade decorations, including tree-top angels and decorated Christmas trees.

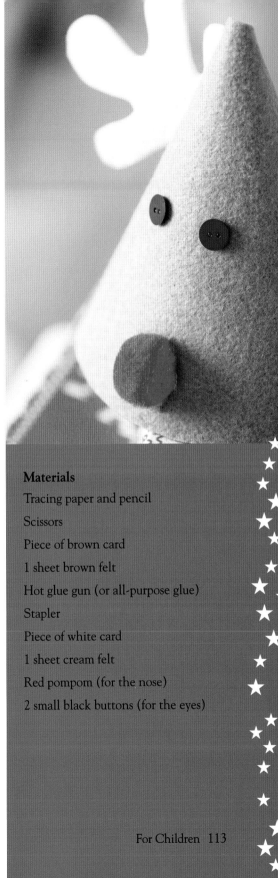

1 Using the templates on page 120, enlarge or trace the cone and antler shapes onto the paper. Cut out both shapes with the scissors. Stick the piece of brown card onto the felt with the glue or a glue gun, and allow to dry. Place the semi-circular cone template on top of the card and cut out with scissors.

2 Roll the semi-circle of brown card and felt into a neat cone shape and then fix into position using the stapler. You will need to use several staples to keep the shape firmly fixed in place.

Materials
Tracing paper and pencil
Scissors
Piece of brown card
1 sheet brown felt
Hot glue gun (or all-purpose glue)
Stapler
Piece of white card
1 sheet cream felt
Red pompom (for the nose)
2 small black buttons (for the eyes)

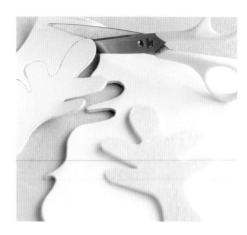

3 Glue the piece of white card to the the cream-colored felt using the glue or a glue gun, and allow to dry. Place the antler template on top of the card and cut out two antlers using the scissors.

4 Glue the two antler shapes to the back of the cone near the pointed end. You may find it quicker to do this with a hot glue gun if you have one.

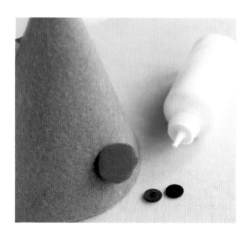

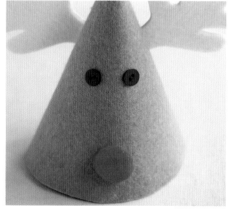

5 Carefully glue the bright red pompom to the front of the cone in order to make the reindeer's nose.

6 To finish, glue the two button eyes to the cone, approximately 1½in (4cm) above the red pompom nose and about 1¼in (3cm) apart.

Top tip

You can use the cone template to make lots of other Christmas decorations. For example, you might like to make a row of miniature Christmas trees using different shades of green felt instead of brown. Decorate them with tiny red and green beads to look like baubles. Finish off each tree with a felt ball.

Red and white paperchains

Paperchains are always popular with children and they will have great fun linking the chains together for Christmas. Why not give the classic paperchain an original twist by finishing it with a decorative edge and a punched design? Here, I made the paperchains in alternate red and white for a truly festive look.

1 Using the ruler and pencil, mark out the width of the paperchains on the back of the paper and parallel with the shorter edge, making each chain about 1¼in (3cm) wide. (The length of the paperchains will be the same as the paper's shortest side.)

2 Use the decorative edging scissors to cut out each paperchain.

3 Use the festive hole punch to cut out the designs along the paperchain. I used three punched designs per paperchain but you can do more if you wish.

4 Fold the first paperchain to form a loop and glue the ends into place, overlapping them by about ½in (1cm). Thread the second piece of paper through the first loop and glue into position. Continue to thread the paper pieces through the last loop to create the chain, making sure you alternate the colors for each loop. If you are making long lengths of paperchain, you may find it quicker to use a stapler. The staples will be visible but it will save considerable time.

Templates

All templates can be traced and used at the size shown here, apart from the body for the Felt Cone Reindeer and the Starry Silk and Velvet Stocking—these are shown at half their true size, so please photocopy at 200%.

Felt Cone Reindeer (page 112)

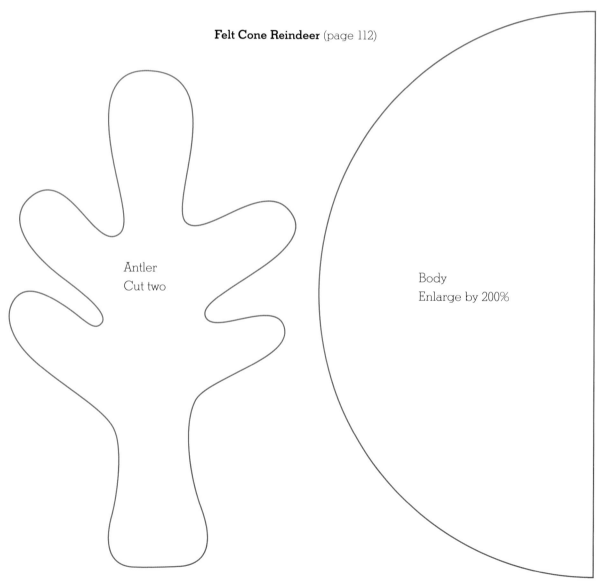

Antler
Cut two

Body
Enlarge by 200%

Starry Silk and Velvet Stocking
Enlarge by 200%
Cut two in silk and one in wadding

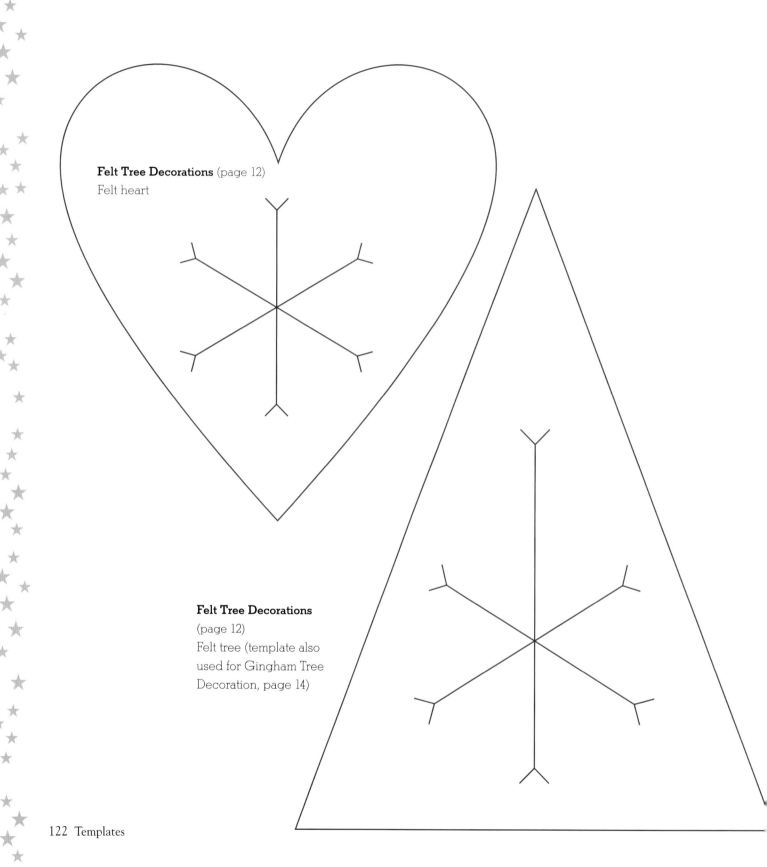

Felt Tree Decorations (page 12)
Felt heart

Felt Tree Decorations
(page 12)
Felt tree (template also
used for Gingham Tree
Decoration, page 14)

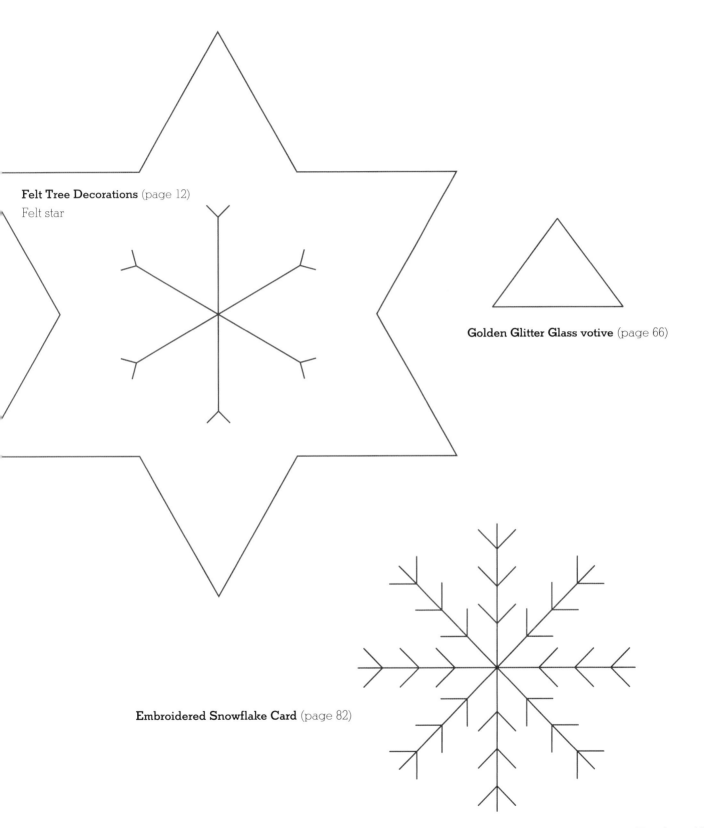

Felt Tree Decorations (page 12)
Felt star

Golden Glitter Glass votive (page 66)

Embroidered Snowflake Card (page 82)

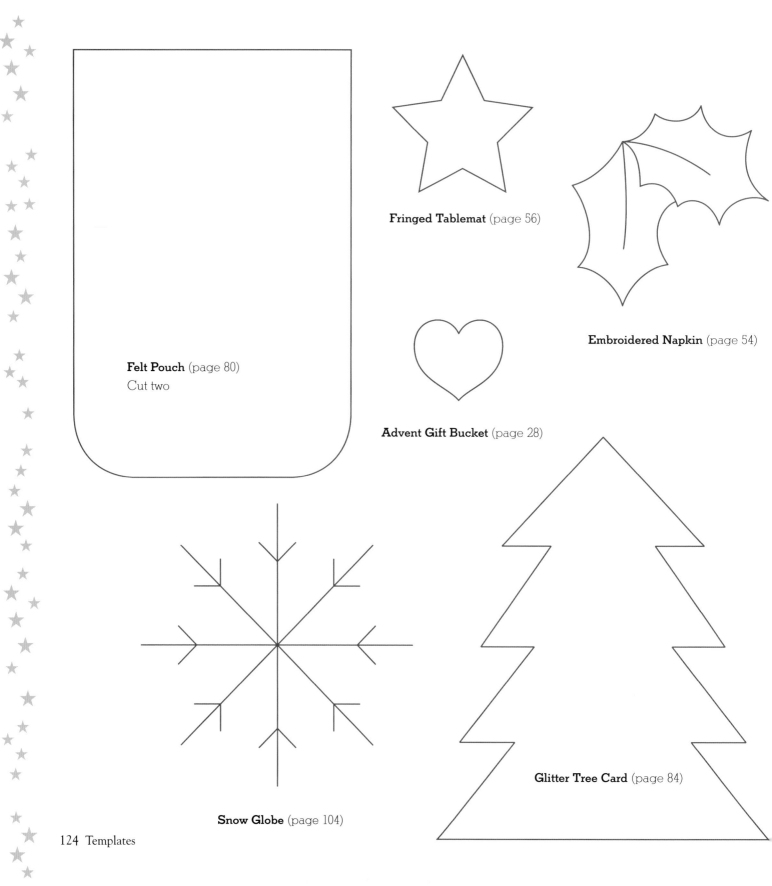

Fringed Tablemat (page 56)

Embroidered Napkin (page 54)

Felt Pouch (page 80)
Cut two

Advent Gift Bucket (page 28)

Glitter Tree Card (page 84)

Snow Globe (page 104)

Suppliers

UNITED STATES

A. C. Moore
www.acmoore.com
Arts and crafts superstore stocking different papers, decorative beads, and stamps, as well as scrapbooking supplies.

Britex Fabrics
www.britexfabrics.com
Online supplier of excellent range of fabrics, buttons, lace, ribbons, notions.

Create for Less
www.createforless.com
Large selection of craft, needlework, and sewing supplies, including beads, buttons, decorative flowers, felt, and ribbons.

Darice
www.darice.com
Extensive range of art and craft supplies, including felt, pompoms, sequins, buttons, ribbons, glitters, glues, and paints.

Hobby Lobby
www.hobbylobby.com
Excellent selection of sewing supplies, notions, ribbons, trims, and buttons.

Ikea
www.ikea.com/us
Superstore with a good range of home-decoration, fabric, and baking supplies.

Jo-Ann Fabrics & Crafts
www.joann.com
Wide selection of fabric, sewing, and craft supplies, as well as jewelry-making materials and beads.

Michaels
www.michaels.com
Good range of sewing, needlework, and craft materials.

M&J Trimming
www.mjtrim.com
Lovely selection of decorative trims, notions, ribbons, lace, and buttons.

The Home Depot
www.homedepot.com
Good selection of home-decorating supplies, including paints and fabrics, and tools such as glue guns.

UNITED KINGDOM

Beading In London
(formerly known as Ells & Farrier)
www.beadinginlondon.co.uk
Huge selection of jewelry-making materials, plus feathers, sequins, and wood, glass, pearl, and crystal beads.

Calico Crafts
www.calicocrafts.co.uk
Online specialist with a large stock of crafting materials, as well as birch ply boxes ready for decorating and vintage-style labels for découpage projects.

Cath Kidston
Visit www.cathkidston.co.uk for details of your nearest store.
Pretty, vintage-style fabrics sold by the yard.

Cox & Cox
www.coxandcox.co.uk
Mail-order and online catalog with a good selection of ribbons and wrapping, plus unusual items such as wooden parcel labels.

Creations Art and Craft Materials
www.ecreations.co.uk
Online craft store with a large stock of modeling clay, simple stitchcraft, stencils, paints, brushes, glues, and more.

Dunelm Mill
www.dunelm-mill.com
Crafting materials such as paints and paintbrushes, blank MDF shapes for decorating, and paper; haberdashery items like ribbons and buttons; and fabrics, sewing thread, and blank cards

Hobbycraft
Visit www.hobbycraft.co.uk for details of your nearest store.
Chain of superstores stocking a massive selection of art and craft materials

Homecrafts Direct
www.homecraftsdirect.co.uk
Ideal for craft staples such as crêpe paper and fabric paints, as well as for hard-to-find items such as balsa wood and cement

Ikea

Visit www.ikea.com for a catalogue or details of your nearest store.
Good selection of seasonal decorations, wrapping paper, and cards, as well as wooden boxes and plain picture frames for painting and decorating.

Jane Asher Party Cakes and Sugarcraft

www.jane-asher.co.uk
Excellent selection of novelty cookie cutters, plus cake frills, paper doilies, and colored cake cases in different sizes.

John Lewis

www.johnlewis.com
Includes a good haberdashery department stocking fabrics, felt, wools, ribbons, and decorative beads and trims, as well as blank cards with envelopes.

Lakeland

Visit www.lakelandlimited.com for details of your nearest store.
Mail-order and online supplier of fantastic craft products, including decorative stamps and inks, plus cake- and sweet-making accessories.

MacCulloch & Wallis

www.macculloch-wallis.co.uk
Great selection of fabrics and sewing threads, as well as lace, ribbons, ric rac and other braids, buttons, and appliqué motifs.

Paperchase

Visit www.paperchase.co.uk for details of your nearest store.
Handmade papers, crêpe and tissue paper, card, plus blank cards and envelopes in many colors and sizes.

The Craft Sewer

www.craftysewer.com
A sewing and craft superstore with a wide selection of craft materials, including buttons, beads, sequins, pompoms, felt, wool, and blank cards, as well as cake-decorating items such as frosting (icing), food colorings, and decorations.

The English Stamp Company

www.englishstamp.com
Great range of traditional wooden stamps and printing inks, including Christmas-themed stamps in various sizes.

The Stencil Library

www.stencil-library.com
Decorative stencils, from simple shapes to complicated all-over designs, as well as water-based stencil paints and brushes.

VV Rouleaux

Visit www.vvrouleaux.com for details of your nearest store.
A vast selection of ribbons from taffeta and velvet to embroidered cotton, plus beaded motifs, pompoms, pretty trims, feather birds, and fabric flowers.

Acknowledgements

A huge thank you to Caroline Arber for her lovely photography for the book and to Gillian Haslam for her enthusiasm and guidance!
Thanks are also due to Dunelm Mill, Hobbycraft, and The English Stamp Company for providing the lovely crafting products used extensively throughout the book.
And, as always, thank you to my husband Michael and daughters, Jessica and Anna, for their help and support, and for putting up with the all the mess I make while crafting madly!

Index